50p

chanzy

Orchids

Wonders of Nature

Orchids

— TAKASHI KIJIMA —

Wonders of
Nature

a Salamander book

Published by Salamander Books Limited
LONDON • NEW YORK

Published by Salamander Books Ltd,
52 Bedford Row,
London WC1R 4LR
United Kingdom

Photographs by Takashi Kijima
Text by Yoshio Udagawa and Takashi Kijima

© 1987 Takashi Kijima
© 1987 Shogakukan, Tokyo
© 1988 Fenice 2000 for International Edition

ISBN 0 86101 422 7

All correspondence concerning the content of this
volume should be addressed to Salamander Books Ltd.

Distributed by:
Hodder and Stoughton Services,
PO Box 6, Mill Road, Dunton Green,
Sevenoaks, Kent TN13 2XX

Printed in Italy

Contents

L
ooking at picture books, children lose track of time as they become absorbed in the drama unfolding page-by-page. This photo collection was organized as a "picture book for adults," who, harassed by the accelerating pace of life, sometimes need to partake of the childlike and forget time.

From my male viewpoint, the wild orchids in this picture book all seem feminine. Among the photographs here, we find the meeting of the sperm and the egg, the fetus, the infant, and the mischievous little girl. Present also are the prim maiden, the wild extroverted girl, the demure matron, and the captivating beauty. One could easily write a script from this that would resemble a real human drama.

Humans, after all, are not the only beings who live dramatic lives. All things living on Earth play out the drama of reproduction to assure the survival of their species. They create through the dramatic arts of their genetic codes. Those who give a poor performance die out; those with good stagecraft survive. Such is the history of species.

But what about the ladies who take the stage in this collection? They appeared much earlier than human beings, nearly two hundred million years ago, and have not just survived, but have spread from the equator to the Arctic Circle, from the Himalayan plateau to the plains, and number species in the tens of thousands. The dramatic arts of these ladies have not been only successful, but give us stories of mystery and subtle intrigue.

They have a glamorous energy that appeals to us humans, who fancy ourselves the lords of creation. These sometimes narcissistic, sometimes eccentric ladies reveal themselves carelessly; they stand out among all flowering plants with their strangely appealing personalities; they display a mysterious capacity for infinite change; they seem to hide an enigma.

Their enigmatic dramatic arts have been personified and gathered together in this photo collection, which is divided into three sections according to theme. The first is arranged to suggest a woman's life. Images of girlhood through mature womanhood are presented, as well as those showing conception, joy, mischievousness… The second section is arranged to display the "progress of the species," seen through the eyes of the photographer. Forms appear that suggest images of primitive and modern man, including changes, variations, and transformations. The third is an attempt to present the underlying "mystery of creation".

"Creation" is a word that can only be used appropriately by a creator. Perhaps the mystery we see in the figures of these lovely ladies can help us slow down our lives and become creators ourselves.

Takashi Kijima

The Origins of Orchids and a Fascination for Form

To the eyes of science, all orchids' secrets have been disclosed. At least as far as the lucid coldness of science can go… Though, there seems to be something still unrevealed, something almost impossible to express. Photographer Takashi Kijima, with his visual sensitivity, has drawn near this mysterious and essential core.

His images do not just record the external forms of orchids, but, through orchids, approach the true image of nature and explore its inner recesses to draw forth what might be called its essence. This collection of photographs, organized like a suggestive riddle, has an element of mystery. What is the appeal of orchids, the fascination that lies at the base of Kijima's artistic vision? Before explaining the three main themes – personification, genesis, and flux – I would like to trace the origins and forms of orchids.

Orchids are far older than man. Fossils of some have been found that date from the time between the Jurassic period of the Mesozoic era (from 195 to 136 million years ago) and the Cenozoic period (64 million years ago). The relationship between men and orchids is thought to have probably begun on the coast of the Mediterranean Sea, where *Orchis* and *Ophrys* grow wild, or possibly in the China that produced Peking Man.

The first recorded mention of orchids is found in *Enquiry Into Plants*, written by Theophrastus, a student of Aristotle, around 300 B.C. They were first identified clearly as "orchids" in the first century A.D. by Dioscorides, a Greek medicinal botanist whose *Materia Medica* was a standard reference until the Middle Ages. In Asia, the great philosopher and statesman Confucius kept orchids in his rooms, and wrote a poem praising their fragrance.

Orchidaceae, or *Orchid*, as it is called in English, was known to the Greeks as *orchis* two thousand years ago. This is said to refer to *Orchis morio*, which can still be seen in that region. The name means "testicle," for rather obvious reasons.

The present Western orchid got its start during the Great Age of Navigation, when it was brought to Europe with other trade goods from the "savage" tropics. The first to reach Europe, in 1731, is said to have been the *Bletia verecunda*, a wild orchid discovered on the island of Providence in the West Indies.

In the 19th century it became easier to import orchids from the tropics, and advances in glass manufacturing facilitated the construction of greenhouses. These developments fueled the enthusiasm of the wealthy and the aristocracy for orchid cultivation as they competed to collect rare and beautiful specimens. Although many exploration parties of aristocrats and scholars left for unexplored tropical regions, the largest contribution to orchid collecting was probably made by orchid hunters employed by the orchid traders. These loners labored months or years at the risk of their lives. Although the rewards were great if they found outstanding specimens, many met with a tragic fate after a long and lonely journey. The Skinner *(Skinneri)* is one of the many whose names have been passed down over the centuries to commemorate orchid hunters.

Over the years, many scholars participated in naming and classifying the growing number of orchids brought from the tropics, and left behind a record of substantial achievement. The cultivation of new varieties, begun in the latter half of the 19th century, made rapid advances and produced an enormous number of types. The registration system of the Royal Horticultural Society has been continued down to the present day, and remains unequalled in the world of floriculture.

What is it about orchids that makes them so appealing? Color, brilliance, shape…? Of monocotyledon plants, the brilliance of the orchid can be found only in the ginger family. Another distinctive feature is that the stamens are united with the pistils to form what is known as the column.

This column is clearly exposed in some flowers, and hidden in the labellum in others. Kijima used soft focus to photograph flowers with exposed columns, perhaps to give the image of the exposed column a sexual element. In contrast to many orchids that expose thick columns, the maidenly *Laelia* demurely encloses hers in the lobe of the sepal. Flowers are basically reproductive organs, and the Creator may have displayed them so beautifully as a contrast to human beings. Even so, gentle flowers also hide the sexual arts of deception deep in their inner recesses.

The relationship between orchids and insects is a fascinating one. The orchid has developed various distinctive ploys to facilitate pollination by insects. For example, orchids usually put forth androgynous flowers, but some have separate male and female flowers. The *Catasetum*, which grows in Central America, has a male flower that possesses a tactile sense. When the flower is touched by insect feet, a spray of pollen flies up, sometimes over a meter high, to stick firmly to the insect's back. The *Ophrys* and the *Drakaea* assume the forms of female insects, and exchange pollen through the mating movements of deceived males. These seductive arts have a charm that is definitely unplantlike.

The minute seeds are also surprising. One seed pod contains from tens to hundreds of thousands of seeds, which are light enough to be carried hundreds of kilometers by the wind. And Nature has arranged it so that the seeds will not bud without the help of mycorrhizal fungi.

The more we learn about orchids, the more mysterious their nature becomes. Approaching the wonders of Nature and her extreme profusion of forms through this photographic collection, one's sense of wonder is deeply aroused.

Yoshio Udagawa

Daughters
The whisperings of a new day with the dawn sky brightening from the east, but the deep sleep remains undisturbed. The daughters' dreaming faces reveal their utter youthfulness. The drowsy, sleepy *Habenaria rhodocheila* is in the spell of the whistling Pan, the goat god, and could it be that they are having a dream about dancing with the young? Perhaps it is the dream of *Habenaria columbae* dressed in robes of white carrying a cross on his back. The sun has begun to rise. Just as the cheerful singing of Eros, the god of love, can be heard, the *Comparettia* begins to open its skirts and take up the rhythm. This is the first sign of the daughters waking.

A bemused smile
When looking at *Cattleya* orchids one can't help think of the bemused face of the Mona Lisa. It is believed that even having spent three years on his masterpiece, Leonardo da Vinci died unsatisfied with his work and was still in the process of making changes. It is a painting of elegance and sensual beauty stirring up excitement in the onlooker and at the same time imparting an image of freshness. It is thought that da Vinci painted while having his subject listen to music. I wonder how it would be if we had the *Cattleya* listen to music. Perhaps the waltz for *warneri* and the mazurka for *coerulea*.

Thoughts of the womb
Lycaste are most certainly not ladies of the gentry. Even though they publicly display their reproductive act they are far beyond contempt. *Lycaste* conjure up an image of the scene beneath the heavily laden orange tree in Botticelli's painting "Spring" where a gathering of angels and nymphs surround the figure of Venus. The beauty of the barefooted Flora, the goddess of flowers, and the rhythm of the skimpily dressed dancing bodies appear to be in keeping with the *Lycaste*'s rhythm. It seems that it is this healthy, elegant nakedness that characterizes and draws attention to orchids.

Habenaria (abbrev. *Hab.*)
The name means bridle reins derived from the sepal formation which hang down like leather straps. This is one of the large genera of terrestrial orchids with some 750 species found in a wide area from the tropical to the temperate zones of the world. During the winter, the stem and flower die off and the roots remain dormant.

Comparettia (abbrev. *Comp.*)
This genus takes its name from the Italian botanist A. Comparetti. It consists of about 12 kinds of small, epiphytic (using other plants to grow on for support only) orchids, found in the Andes and northern part of South America. Small bulbs, leathery leaves, long stalks, and pretty clusters of flowers are the main characteristics of this genus.

Cattleya (abbrev. *C.*)
The name is derived from the name of the British orchid collector W. Cattley. There are about 65 species of this genus of epiphytic orchid found in the tropics of South America; in particular Brazil. This is a typical genus of Occidental orchids with many of the species characterized by beautiful flowers.

Lycaste (abbrev. *Lyc.*)
This is the name of a nymph in Greek mythology and was also the name of the beautiful daughter of Priam, the last king of Troy. This genus consists of about 40 species spread over a wide area from Mexico to Brazil. Some of the species are epiphytic and others are semiterrestrial. The flowers are distinctive for the large triangular shape of the sepals.

Following data is given below the species in this and in all chapters: Place of origin / Flowering size / Blooming season.

1. *Lyc. skinneri* var. *alba*
Mexico and Guatemala / 12-15 cm / Winter to spring

2. *C. warneri* var. *alba*
Brazil / 15 cm / Early summer

3. *Hab. rhodocheila*
Southeast Asia / 2 × 4 cm / Autumn

4. *Hab. columbae*
Thailand and Laos / 2.5 cm / Autumn

5. *Comp. speciosa*
Ecuador / 3 cm / Autumn to winter

6. *C. bowringiana* var. *coerulea*
Honduras and Guatemala / 6-8 cm / Summer to autumn

7. *Comp. macroplectron*
Colombia / 4 × 5 cm / Winter to spring

8. *C. citrina* = *Encyclia citrina*
In the mountains of Mexico (above 1500 m) / 10 cm / Spring to summer

9. *C. violacea*
From Colombia to Peru and Brazil / 10 cm / Summer

10. *C. walkeriana*
Brazil / 10 cm / Winter to spring

11. *Lyc. cochleata*
From Mexico to Guatemala / 5 cm / Spring

12. *Lyc. deppei*
Mexico and Guatemala / 7-10 cm / Late spring

13. *Lyc. ciliata*
On high ground in Colombia and Peru / 6-10 cm / Winter

14. *Lyc. lasioglossa*
Guatemala and Honduras / 10 cm / January to March

2

The Conception and Joy of Life

Images of the Fetus and Infant

Suggestions
The *Cadetia* are similar to ovaries and the *Angraecopsis* resemble spermatozoa. The *Anguloa* is born quietly in the womb rather like an embryo child. For such a performance the stage should be set with a splendid array of seven colors and a joyful oratorio. The *Megaclinium* walk along with a heavy gait and the *Gomesa*, although capable of walking, dances along in a frenzied fashion while trying to blossom out. It seems appropriate to offer up the prayer, "What no eye has seen, nor ear heard, nor the heart of man conceived, what God has prepared for those who love him," quoted in The First Letter to the Corinthians to these small blossoming children. Just as things are becoming as still as death, there is a sudden movement as if a box of toys has been overturned. The stillness in movement and the movement in the stillness is because of the small children.

Mental energy of flowers
Truth is reality, reality is life, and life is the central memory of nature. This kind of concept comes in unseen waves of mental energy which are then communicated to others. Whenever there is a point of contact for these waves of energy the shutter drops down. This is termed as the determining instant and it is not the kind of concept understood by the animal or plant world when they appear in front of the camera. Because these flowers are small they move but only slightly and it is the sun's rays that amplify these delicate waving motions. This is probably because somehow they possess a primitive memory directly relating to the movement of the sun. I have strong feelings about taking photographs of these small flowers bathing in sunlight.

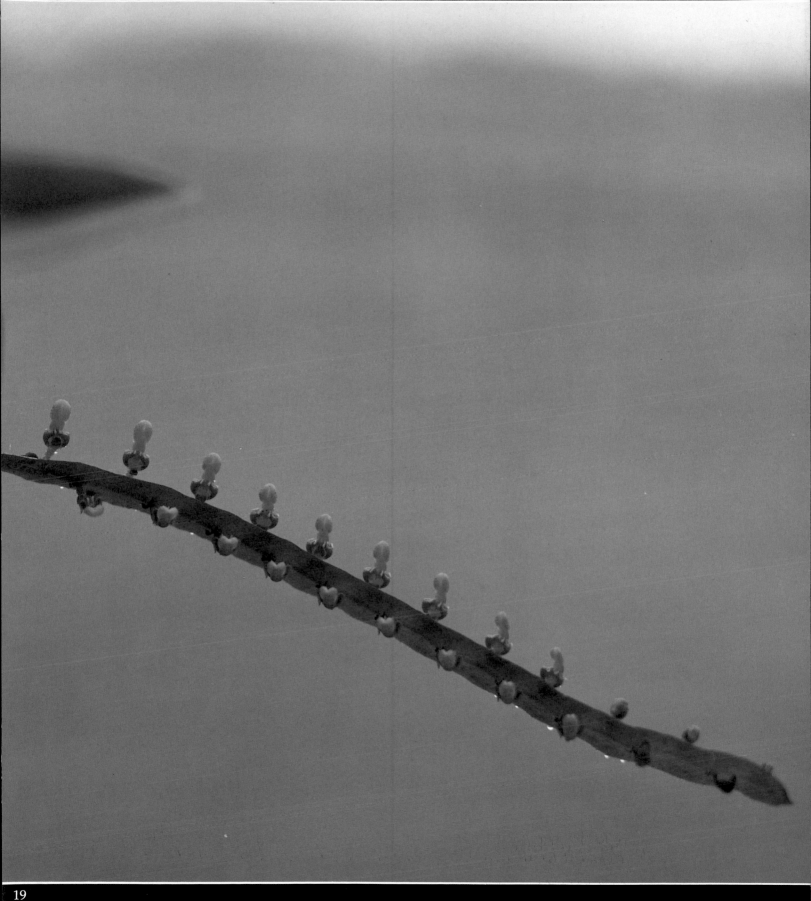

22

23

Cadetia

This genus commemorates the name of Cadet de Gassicourt. There are about 50 species in this genus of small epiphytic orchids found in New Guinea and Southeast Asia. The stalk grows stiffly upright with a single terminal leaf. The roots form in thick clusters and the flowers are small and of a unique shape.

Angraecopsis

The name infers that the plants of this genus are similar in shape to the *Angraecum*. This genus comprises small, epiphytic orchids with between 10 and 14 species that grow in Madagascar and the tropical parts of Africa. Mainly with short stems supporting a few leaves. The flower stems droop down, bearing clusters of small white flowers.

Anguloa (abbrev. *Ang.*)

English name–cradle orchid

This genus takes its name from the Spanish botanist Angulo. There are about 10 species of these large, sometimes epiphytic, sometimes terrestrial orchids. They can be found mainly in the mountainous areas of northern South America. The stem and leaves are similar to *Lycaste*, but the spherical flowers do not completely open out.

Bulbophyllum (abbrev. *Bulb.*)
= *Megaclinium*

The name is a combination of the Latin for bulb and Greek for leaf. This is the largest of the orchid genera with more than 1000 species identified over a very wide area of the world's tropical, subtropical, and temperate zones. They are epiphytic orchids and although the distinctive, flat-stalked species were previously classified in *Megaclinium*, the tendency now is for them all to be included in the same group.

Gomesa

This genus has been named after the Portuguese army doctor and botanist B.A. Gomes. There are about 10 species of this small, epiphytic orchid to be found in Brazil. The yellowy green flowers are arranged in thick rows.

Gongora

This genus has taken the name of C. Gongora, the one-time governor-general of New Granada. The 12 or so species are epiphytic and grow in Southern and Central America from Brazil to Mexico. These richly flowering orchids hang down with each flower resembling the open wings of an insect.

Jumellea

This genus is named after the French botanist H. Jumelle. The different species are found in Madagascar and the neighboring islands. There are some 50 species, some of which are epiphytic and some lithophytic, i.e., growing among rocks and on rock surfaces. The petals and sepals are long and thin and the usually single flower is of a distinctive shape.

15. *Cyc. ventricosum*
English name: swan orchid
Mexico to Panama / 10 cm / Mainly summer

16. *Cadetia taylori*
Oceania, mainly Australia / 1-1.2 cm / Irregular

17. *Ang. uniflora = Ang. virginalis*
South America, particularly Colombia / 4 × 6 cm / Late spring

18. *Angraecopsis gracillima*
In the highland forests of Kenya and Uganda / 1 cm / Summer

19. *Bulb. falcatum = Megaclinium falcatum*
From Guinea to Uganda / 0.8 cm (length) / Spring

20. *Gomesa glaziovii*
Brazil / 2 cm / Winter

21. *Gongora galeata*
Mexico / 5 cm / Mainly summer

22. *Jumellea* sp.
____ / ____ / Winter to spring

23. *Eulophidium pulchellum*
____ / 3 cm / ____

24. *Comp. coccinea*
Brazil / 2 cm / Winter

25. *Ctsm. tenebrosum*
Peru / 3 × 5 cm / Spring to summer

26. *Palumbina candida*
Guatemala / 3 cm / Spring

27. *Brs. longissima*
Costa Rica to Colombia / 30 cm / Early summer

28. *Cyc. chlorochilon = Cyc. ventricosum* var. *chlorochilon*
Venezuela and Colombia / 12-15 cm / Summer

29. *Cyc. pentadactylon*
Brazil and Peru / 10 cm / Mainly summer

30. *Chdrh. aromatica*
Costa Rica and Panama / 6 cm / Spring to summer

31. *Ctsm. viridiflavum*
Panama / 8-10 cm / Spring to summer

32. *Cymbidiella rhodochila*
Moss-covered areas in the forests of Madagascar / 6 cm / Spring to summer

Eulophidium
The name comes from these orchids being smaller but similar to the *Eulophia* genus. It is a terrestrial group of orchids found widely in Madagascar and generally in tropical areas. There are about 30 species which are characterized by the stalk growing straight up from the base of the bulbous section and although they are quite plain, the blossoms are usually a variety of colors.

Palumbina
The name is derived from the word for wild pigeon because the shape of the tip of the column resembles the open wings of a pigeon. This is a single species genus found in a particular area of Guatemala. It is epiphytic and quite small with a slender stalk and many distinctive small white flowers.

Catasetum (abbrev. *Ctsm.*)
The name is a composite of the two notions of lower and hairy thorn, used to describe the antenna of the male part of the flower. There are about 100 different species of this orchid to be found in tropical America. They are epiphytic plants with separate male and female flowers. The pollen is released as if sprung open when the male antenna is touched.

Brassia (abbrev. *Brs.*)
The name comes from W. Brass, a botanical painter. These orchids are epiphytic and the 30 or so species can be found across a wide part of Central and South America. The stalk grows quite long and the perianth lobe is long and slender. The blossoms grow in bunches and because they resemble spiders in shape they are sometimes referred to as "spider orchids."

Cycnoches (abbrev. *Cyc.*)
The name is a combination of the words for swan and neck which describes the curved shape of the stamen. There are between 7 and 12 species to be found in most parts of an area from Mexico to Brazil. They are epiphytic orchids with considerable variety even among the same species. They are bisexual flowers usually with large, beautiful blooms.

Cochleanthes
= *Chondrorhyncha* (abbrev. *Chdrh.*)
These orchids resemble small bird's beaks, which together with the word for cartilage gives them their name. They are epiphytic and the 12 species can be found in the relatively cooler parts of the American tropics. The flowers are typically dark purples and greens on a white base.

Cymbidiella
The name literally translated means small *Cymbidium*. These are epiphytic orchids only occurring in Madagascar and only three species have so far been identified. The stalk and leaves are very similar to the *Cymbidium* genus of orchids but when in bloom they are quite different. Although not particularly large, they are distinctive in color and shape.

3

The Mischievous Age
Images of Young Children

A child's sentiments
Children grow and change while feeding on the energy of nature. An unknown strength is hidden in their incomplete make-up. If one were to try and depict this sentiment by identifying it with an orchid, I wonder which one would be the most appropriate. The *Bulbophyllum* trying to fly into the sky, the *Masdevallia* always striving to be taller, the *Maxillaria* taking care not to let its tongue hang out, or the unsophisticated *Chysis* eternally hoping to be a beauty. They are all mischievous, energetic little blossoms. No amount of chiding would have any effect, they will continue to do just as they please.

37

38

39

40

41

42

43

45

44

46

47

48

49

50

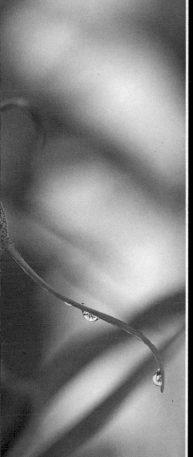

51

Masdevallia (abbrev. *Masd.*)
J. Masdevall, a Spanish botanist, gives his name to this genus which can be found in the northern part of Southern America, especially in the tropical areas of the Andes mountains. They can be epiphytic or terrestrial. The spoon-shaped leaves grow together thickly from which sprout the sepals and distinctive flowers.

Dracula (abbrev. *Drac.*)
Small dragon is the name that has been given to this genus and somehow befits the image of these orchids. There are some 60 species to be found from Colombia and Ecuador up through Central America. They are epiphytic or lithophytic and usually prefer the cooler areas of mist shrouded forests. Before being identified as a separate genus they were regarded as part of *Masdevallia*.

Maxillaria (abbrev. *Max.*)
The name comes from the word jaw because the shape of the stamen and the labellum of some varieties resembles the jaw of an insect. The 300 different species of this epiphytic orchid can be found over a wide area of Central and South America from Argentina up as far as southern Florida. They are single flower orchids usually quite plain and small but many of them give off a pleasant fragrance.

Chysis (abbrev. *Chys.*)
The name comes from the word meaning to fuse and appears to refer to the method of pollen dispersal that takes place in the pollinium. The different species, about six all told, are epiphytic and can be seen from Mexico to Venezuela and Peru. The roots are fleshy and spindleshaped and usually droop downwards. The medium size flowers are of a fleshy substance and glossy in appearance.

33. *Masd. ignea = Masd. militaris*
In the high mountains of Colombia between 2500 and 3500 m / 4-6 cm / Spring

34. *Bulb. refractum*
Mainly the Himalayas and Thailand / 5 cm (length) / Spring

35. *Bulb. dearei*
Borneo and the Philippines / 6 cm / Summer

36. *Bulb. caespitosum*
Sikkim / 2 cm (length) / Early spring

37. *Masd. coccinea*
In the mountains of Colombia and Peru between 2400 and 3100 m / 4 × 6 cm / Spring

38. *Drac. astuta*
Costa Rica / 3-5 cm / Winter to spring

39. *Masd. wurdackii*
Peru / 4 × 6 cm (excluding the tail piece, the tail piece is approx. 8 cm) / Winter

40. *Max. camaridii*
Tropical Central and South America / 3 cm / Winter

41. *Masd. floribunda*
Mexico / 1.5 cm / Autumn

42. *Masd. infracta*
Brazil and Peru / 1.8 cm / Spring to summer

43. *Max. marginata*
Brazil / 4 cm / Spring

44. *Max. vitelliniflora*
Brazil / 10 cm (half-open) / Spring

45. *Max. sp.*
_____ / _____ / _____

46. *Drac. chimaera*
Colombia / 5-6 cm (excluding the tail petals) / Spring to summer

47. *Masd. caudata*
Mainly Venezuela and Colombia / 3.5 cm (excluding the tail piece, the tail piece is approx. 6 cm) / Spring

48. *Max. houtteana*
Mexico and Guatemala / 4 cm / May to October

49. *Masd. tovarensis*
Venezuela / 2.5 x 8 cm / Winter

50. *Masd. triangularis*
Venezuela and Colombia / 6 cm (including the tail-like section) / Spring

51. *Max. luteo-alba*
Costa Rica, Panama and Colombia / 8 cm / Spring

52. *Chys. laevis*
Mexico and Costa Rica / 6-8 cm / Spring to summer

53. *Bulb. sikkimense*
The Himalayas, especially Sikkim / 1.5-2 cm / Winter to spring

54

4

The Debutante

Images of the Change from Child to Adult

White dress

The *Laelia* is a young maiden on the verge of womanhood. Almost as if it is their first appearance on stage the *Laelia* are clothed in white evening dresses. The frills of their dresses ride up and tickle the skin as the young ladies waltz around the dance floor. Their faces become flushed. "I desire an intense life, for I want to be passionately in love" is the message that the *Laelia purpurata* conveys with its white labellum and red center, a color scheme that would be best displayed on a white background. My feeling is that the mixture of nature's white with the white of the labellum creates a sense of purity.

58   59

Laelia (abbrev. *L.*)
The name is believed to be either that of one of the Vestal Virgins, therefore meaning purity, or from one of the female members of the Laelius family, an aristocratic family of ancient Rome. This genus is very similar to *Cattleya*, but the *Laelia* orchids have a total of eight pollinia compared with four of the *Cattleya* and the other main difference is that the split section of the labellum usually surrounds the stamen.

Schomburgkia (abbrev. *Schom.*)
The German botanist R. Schomburgk lends his name to this genus. There are about 12 species spread through the American tropics from Brazil to Mexico. These large epiphytic orchids are similar to *Laelia* but they have long stalks decorated with undulations of flowers at the ends.

54. *L. crispa*
Brazil / 12 cm / Summer

55. *L. purpurata*
The rocky coastline of southern Brazil / 10-15 cm / May to July

56. *L. rupestris*
Brazil / 5-6 cm / Winter to spring

57. *L. crispilabia*
Brazil / 5 cm / Winter

58. *L. blumenscheinii*
Espirito Santo, Brazil / 4-5 cm / Summer

59. *L. flaba*
Brazil / 5 cm / Mainly spring

60. *L. harpophylla*
Brazil / 7-8 cm / Winter

61. *L. autumnalis*
Mexico / 8-10 cm / Winter

62. *L. perrinii*
Brazil / 10 cm / Autumn

63. *Schom. lueddemanii*
Venezuela, Costa Rica and Panama / 7-8 cm / Unknown

64. *L. gouldiana*
Mexico / 7-8 cm / Winter

65. *Schom. superbiens* var. *quesnelliana*
The highlands of Guatemala and Honduras / 8-10 cm / Autumn

From primitive to modern man
According to geophysicists' theories, all the land masses of the world were as one in aeons past. It should then be possible to find the same species of orchid on the east coast of Africa and on the west coast of India. As a matter of fact, though, it is not known when *Dendrobium*'s ancestors first arrived on the Earth.
The varieties of this orchid are in fact countless, with numerous kinds of leaf shapes to be found: some looking like sponges, some newly sprouted buds, some like pointed spears, and others are rounded like drums. The naked flowers are painted with the primary colors and although it is possible to consider this as the elegant simplicity of a lady, it seems to be more analogous to primitive man. Looking at the various species of the *Dendrobium* is somewhat like looking at an abridged version of the human species.

The labellum "temptress"
Insects are enticed by the hairy labella of these flowers, leaving us to ponder as to why. Perhaps the similarity to the heterogeneous world could explain some of the secrets of that unknown subject, but somehow it is actually different. The transparent colored labellum surrounded by the soft petals when seen in the morning sun looks just like fluff, but rather than displaying an air of cuteness, it is somewhat pitiable. In comparison with other plants that do not have such a fluffy labellum, it is almost as if the *Dendrobium* were narcissistic.

68

69

71

72

73

77

78

79

80

82

83

84

85

86

87

88

89

90

Dendrobium (abbrev. *Den.*)
The name is derived from words meaning woods and shrubs. These epiphytic orchids can be found in an area stretching from the Himalayas to the islands of Oceania, although they are mainly concentrated in Southeast Asia. It is a very large genus with over 1600 species and there have been moves recently to split and reclassify them.

66. *Den. speciosum*
East Australia / 2-3 cm / Spring

67. *Den. finisterrae*
New Guinea / 4-5 cm / Late spring

68. *Den. cucumerium*
Australia / ____ / Mainly spring

69. *Den. distichum*
The Philippines / 1 cm / Summer

70. *Den. anceps*
India, Burma and Thailand / 1 cm / Spring to summer

71. *Den. sp.*
Unknown / ____ / Early spring

72. *Den. sp.*
New Guinea / ____ / Spring

73. *Den. papilio*
The Philippines / 4 cm / Summer

74. *Den. cruentum*
Burma, Thailand and the Malay Peninsula / 4 cm / Autumn

75. *Den. lawesii*
The mountains of New Guinea / 3-4 cm / Irregular

76. *Den. quinquecostatum*
The mountain forests of New Guinea / 3 cm / Summer

77. *Den. taurinum*
Hillsides in the Philippines at about 300 m / 6 cm / Summer

78. *Den. discolor*
Australia and New Guinea / 4-6 cm / Summer

79. *Den. amethystoglossum*
The Philippines / 3-4 cm / Spring

80. *Den. unicum*
Thailand and Laos / 4-5 cm / Spring

81. *Den. miyakei*
Taiwan and the Philippines / 2 cm / Irregular

82. *Den. gratiosissimum*
Burma and Thailand / 7 cm (half-open) / Late spring

83. *Den. chrysanthum*
India, Nepal, Burma and North Thailand / 4 cm / Summer

84. *Den. crepidatum*
Sikkim, Nepal, Burma, and Thailand / 4 cm / Spring

85. *Den. fimbriatum* var. *oculatum*
____ / 5 cm / Spring

86. *Den. primulinum*
From the Himalayas to Burma and Thailand / 6 cm / Spring

87. *Den. hildebrandii*
Low mountain areas of Burma and Thailand / 6 cm / Spring

88. *Den. cochlioides*
The hills of New Guinea between 200 and 400 m / 4 cm / Summer

89. *Den. tetragonum*
Australia / 3 × 9 cm / Spring

90. *Den. lineale* type
New Guinea, New Zealand and the Solomon Islands / 5-7 cm / Autumn to winter

91. *Den. thyrsiflorum*
From the Himalayas to Burma and Thailand / 4 cm / Spring

92. *Den. loddigesii*
Laos and South China / 4-5 cm / Spring

93. *Den. schuetzei*
The Philippines / 6-8 cm / Mainly spring

94. *Den. findlayanum*
Burma and Thailand / 6 cm / Spring

6

Bent, Straight, Spheres and Lines

Variations in the Epidendrum

A wild smell

Epidendrum possess a smell of the wild. Whether it is the stabbing of a finely honed blade or the biting cut of a jagged saw, the feeling is very refreshing. In one of the well-known stories of Greek mythology, Medusa was stripped of her beauty by the goddess Athena for daring to rival the goddess' own good looks. Medusa was made to look so grotesque that any beast or person that should look at her would instantly turn to stone. I wonder how it is with our *Epidendrum medusae*? The *E. ciliare* is a man among men and the *E. glumaceum*, although small in stature, possesses a young man's quick intelligence. The *E. cochleatum* looks all unconcerned dressed in its tailcoat.

97

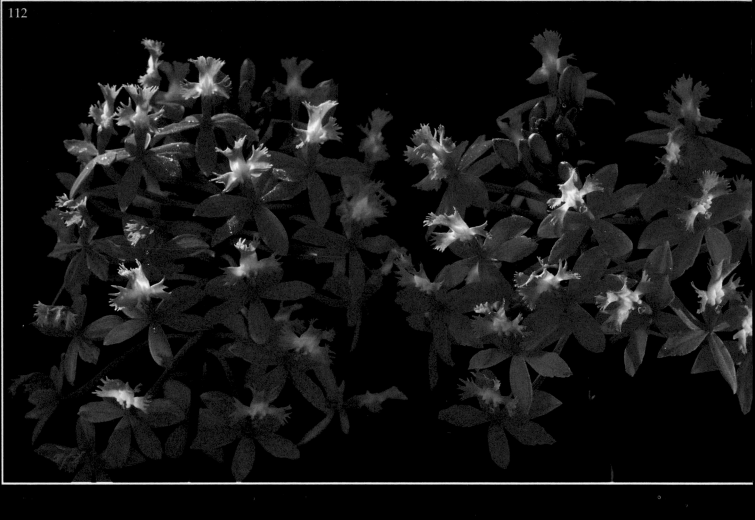

116

117

118

120

121

Epidendrum (abbrev. *Epi.*)
The name is a combination of the words for on and trees and shrubs, stemming from their preference for such woodland hosts. The 1000 or so species come in numerous shapes and can be found in most parts of Central and South America. The blooms are also very variable but usually plain with a few strikingly beautiful variants.

95. *Epi. pseudepidendrum*
Costa Rica and Panama / 6 cm / Summer

96. *Epi. porpax*
Central and northern South America / 2 × 3 cm / Irregular

97. *Epi. sp.*
Ecuador / ____ / ____

98. *Epi. cochleatum*
From Mexico to Brazil / 7-10 cm / Summer

99. *Epi. medusae*
Ecuador / 5 cm / Irregular

100. *Epi. ilense*
West Ecuador / 2.5 × 3 cm / Irregular

101. *Epi. ciliare*
From Mexico to Brazil / 8-12 cm / Summer to autumn

102. *Epi. rigidum*
Tropical and subtropical Central and South America / 2 cm / Summer

103. *Epi. imatophyllum*
From Mexico to Peru and Brazil / 2 cm / Irregular

104. *Epi. atropurpureum* var. *roseum* = *Enc. atropurpureum* var. *rosea*
Tropical America / 5-6 cm / Late spring

105. *Epi. pinniferum*
Southernmost part of Costa Rica / 4 × 5 cm / Summer

106. *Epi. aromaticum*
Tropical America / 5-6 cm / Summer

107. *Epi. selligerum*
Guatemala and Mexico / 4 cm / Winter to spring

108. *Epi. nocturnum*
Tropical America / ____ / Summer

109. *Epi. cinnabarinum*
Northeast Brazil / 6 cm / Spring

110. *Epi. difforme*
From Florida and Mexico to Brazil and Peru / 3 cm / Summer

111. *Epi. glumaceum*
Brazil and Paraguay / 5 cm / Early spring

112. *Epi. radicans* type
From Mexico to Brazil / 2 cm / Uncertain

113. *Epi. stenopetalum*
Central and northern South America / 2.5 cm / Winter to spring

114. *Epi. brassavolae*
Most parts of Central America / 8-10 cm / Late spring

115. *Epi. pseudepidendrum*
Costa Rica and Panama / 6 cm / Summer

116. *Epi. stamfordianum*
Central and northern South America / 3.5 cm / Winter to spring

117. *Epi. prismatocarpum*
Costa Rica and Panama / 5 cm / Summer

118. *Epi. anceps*
Tropical America / 1 cm / Irregular

119. *Epi. allemanoides*
Brazil / 4 cm / Autumn

120. *Epi. vespa*
Tropical America / 2.5 cm / Spring to summer

121. *Epi. coriifolium*
Mexico, Ecuador and Peru / 3 cm / Winter to spring

122. *Epi. stamfordianum*
Central and northern South America / 3.5 cm / Winter to spring

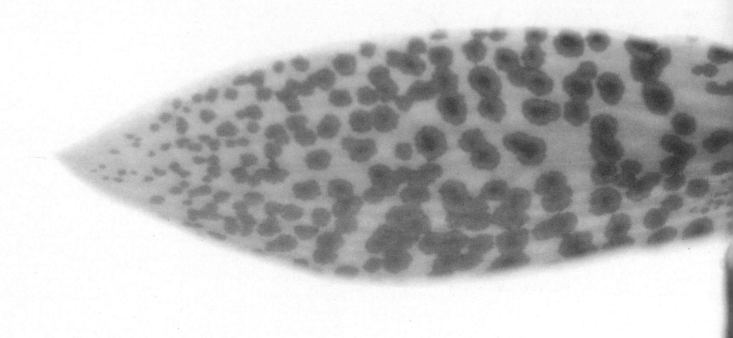

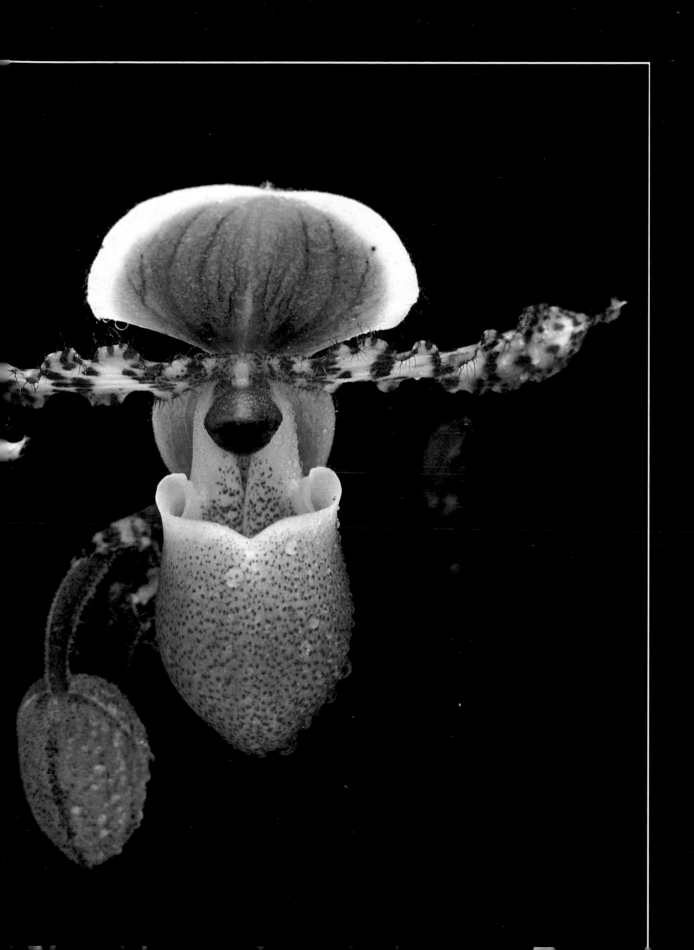

135

136

137

138

139

140

Paphiopedilum (abbrev. *Paph.*)
The name means "sandal of Aphrodite" (of Paphos). There are about 60 different species to be found in an area centered on Southeast Asia stretching from the Himalayas to New Guinea. This genus consists of typical Occidental terrestrial evergreen and semiepiphytic orchids.

Cypripedium (abbrev. *Cyp.*)
The name refers to the footwear of Aphrodite, born, according to Greek mythology, from the sea near Cyprus. This genus of about 35 species can be found all over the world from the tropics to the arctic regions. These terrestrial orchids are similar to *Paphiopedilum* but they are not evergreen, the upper parts of the plant dying off in winter and the lower sections lying dormant.

Phragmipedium (abbrev. *Phrag.*)
The name is derived from the description of the sections of a sandal which refers to these plants having three ovary sections rather than the one of similar genera. There are 10 different species of these terrestrial and semiepiphytic orchids to be found in Central and South America. They are similar to the *Paphiopedilum* genus but the leaves are narrow and thickly clustered and the closely sprouting flowers are in bloom for only a short time.

123. *Paph. sukhakulii*
North Thailand / 12-15 cm / Winter to spring

124. *Cyp. macranthum* var. *hotei-atsumorianum*
Central mountain area of Japan / 6 cm / May

125. *Paph. fairieanum*
The Himalayas, particularly Bhutan and Assam / 6 cm / Spring

126. *Paph. callosum*
Thailand and Cambodia / 10 cm / May to June

127. *Paph. hookerae*
Borneo / 10 cm / Summer

128. *Paph. haynaldianum*
The Philippines / 13-14 cm / Spring

129. *Paph. spicerianum*
Assam / 7 cm / Winter

130. *Paph. dayanum*
Mt. Kinabalu on Borneo / 12 cm / Late spring (April to May)

131. *Paph. chamberlainianum*
Sumatra / 8 cm / Irregular

132. *Phrag. caricinum*
Bolivia and Peru / 5-8 cm / Early summer

133. *Phrag. lindleyanum*
Guyana and Venezuela / 8-10 cm / Winter

134. *Phrag. longifolium*
From Mexico to Colombia and Peru / 15 cm / Summer to autumn

135. *Phrag. caudatum*
From Guatemala and Costa Rica to Colombia and Peru / 60-80 cm (petal length) / Spring to summer

136. *Paph. rothschildianum*
Borneo / 18-28 cm / Spring to summer

137. *Paph. curtisii*
Sumatra / 10-12 cm / Summer

138. *Paph. niveum*
Thailand, Langkawi islands and Pinang island / 6-7 cm / Late spring

139. *Paph. callosum*
Thailand and Cambodia / 10 cm / May to June

140. *Paph. delenatii*
Vietnam / 7-8 cm / Winter

Searching for the Creator's knowledge
The word "Creation" is a word used exclusively, in sacred books, to describe God's making of the heavens and earth. We are taught that we borrow ideas from imagination and originate or create concepts in order to assert our own view of things. Stealing a glance in the direction of the Creator merely reveals that this creation is a fake. It even seems to be just like a plastic flower when it has reached a stage of over cross-fertilization. Among the different genera of orchids that originated long before man ever roamed the planet, it is puzzling to think as to why certain plants should result in such a "plasticity" appearance. Was the Creator merely playing with nature? Or is it the end of a long evolutionary process? Whichever it is, it certainly gives food for thought on the origins of orchids.

Leafless orchid
When looking at the straggly roots of this orchid (*Chiloschista*), it seems to arouse a certain sexual excitement. Is it in memory of the snake that tempted Eve to eat the fruit of the forbidden tree? The way it clings and wraps itself around branches is exactly like the movement of a snake. When the Creator made the forested amusement parks of the world, he also made jungles and decked them with creepers to stop people going in. Maybe the leafless orchid was one of his early experiments. And while still in the development stages, he changed his mind and decided to decorate it with a flower. Perhaps his fascination with the decorative part made him completely forget about adding leaves. Whichever way you look at it the leafless orchid is distinctly primitive. Only the *Trichoglottis philippinensis* seems to dislike its naked appearance and has clothed itself in leaves.

Personification
Somehow or other, the *Oncidium* genus of orchids is very humanlike. The way the *O. phymatochilum* dances about is a real picture of health. In total contrast, the *O. papilio* is quite unsophisticated. It looks like a heavily armored knight from the Crusades looking contemptuously down from under an awe-inspiring helmet, but somehow, something is not quite right. With a deft switch of time this could be old Tokyo, the place was Nihonbashi, the time was the Genroku era: upon the River Sumida, from a floating house-boat Taiko and Shamisen (strings and percussions) are sounding loudly. *O. bicallosum* seems like the Banzuiin-Chobeh, a boss of the Machi-Yakko (City Guardians). And *O. flexuosum* seems one of the group of the Hatamoto-Yakko (roughnecks of Samurai).

Whimsical beauty
The *Brassavola* genus is a relative of the *Cattleya*. The beautiful
princesses of blossoms that decorate the *Cattleya* are neatly and
correctly dressed but those of the *Brassavola* are very individual.
The *Br. nodosa* is dressed with a heart shape and is posed as if
eternally listening for something; the *Br. digbyana* seems to be
happy that it is dressed in the latest fashion with its rustling
labellum; and the *Br. cucullata* stretches its petals out and up as if
trying to join the elite band of female astronauts. It's a very
personal opinion but I am very well disposed towards these ladies
of the *Brassavola* family because, above all, their posturing is ideal
for camerawork.

Yearnings
When the present Emperor was the Crown Prince in the reign of
his father, the flourishing fashion of art nouveau was typified by
an extravagance of curved lines. The Crown Prince was on a royal
visit to Taiwan and upon seeing some white *Phalaenopsis* he
promptly sent a bunch to his wife-to-be. Perhaps those flowers
were *Phalaenopsis amabilis*. I wonder if it was because he associated
these apparently white wings of a dancing butterfly with the future
crown princess. Most certainly the way these flowers flutter would
stir up fond thoughts and yearnings in us all.

Drifting thoughts of an orchid
To think of Orchid, listening to Tohson's famous song "Yashi no
mi" (A Coconut), we cannot help but remember our far distant
ancestors, who were a kind of homeless sea drifting people. This is
why we Japanese are generally fond of Japanese *Ebine*. It is
believed that the *Calanthe* is actually in motion, gradually moving
farther north. In the south the flowers are of a quite complicated
nature but in the east the shapes are quite simple. It was probably
eaten by those very early dwellers in Japan. The seeds themselves
are considered to be the result of 10,000 years of cross-breeding
resulting in a unique blend, a concept that would not be totally out
of place if applied to the Japanese people themselves.

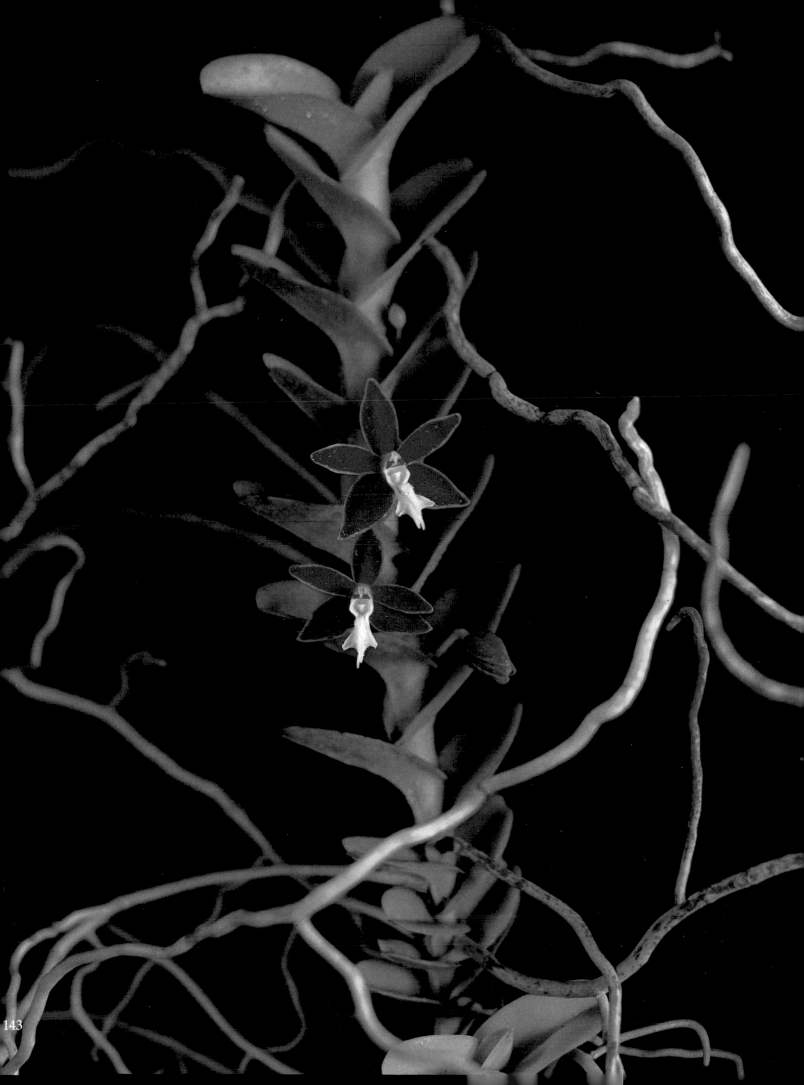

144

145

146   147

153   154

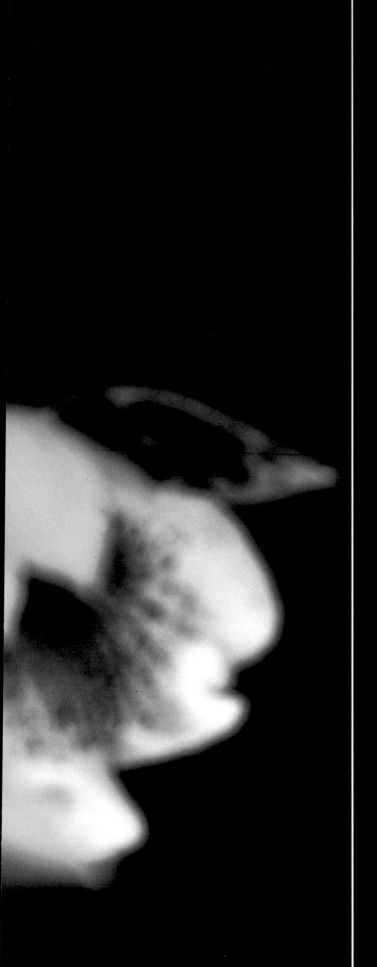

170

171

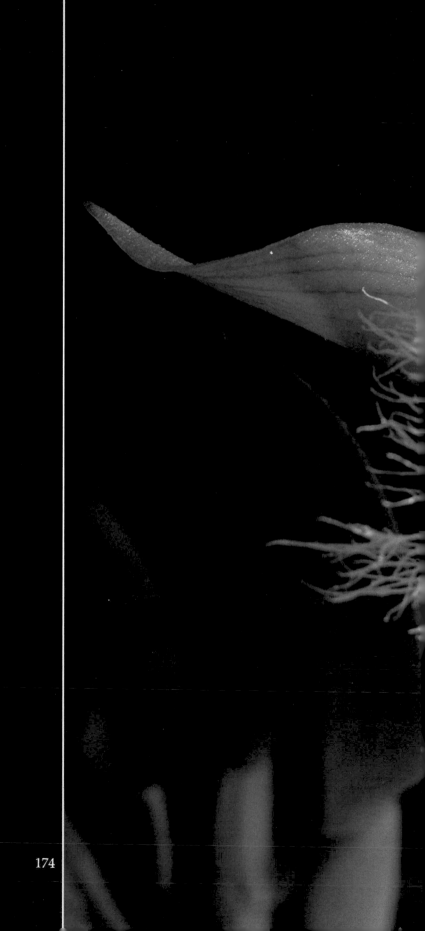

178

179 180

181

182

183

184

185

186

191

193

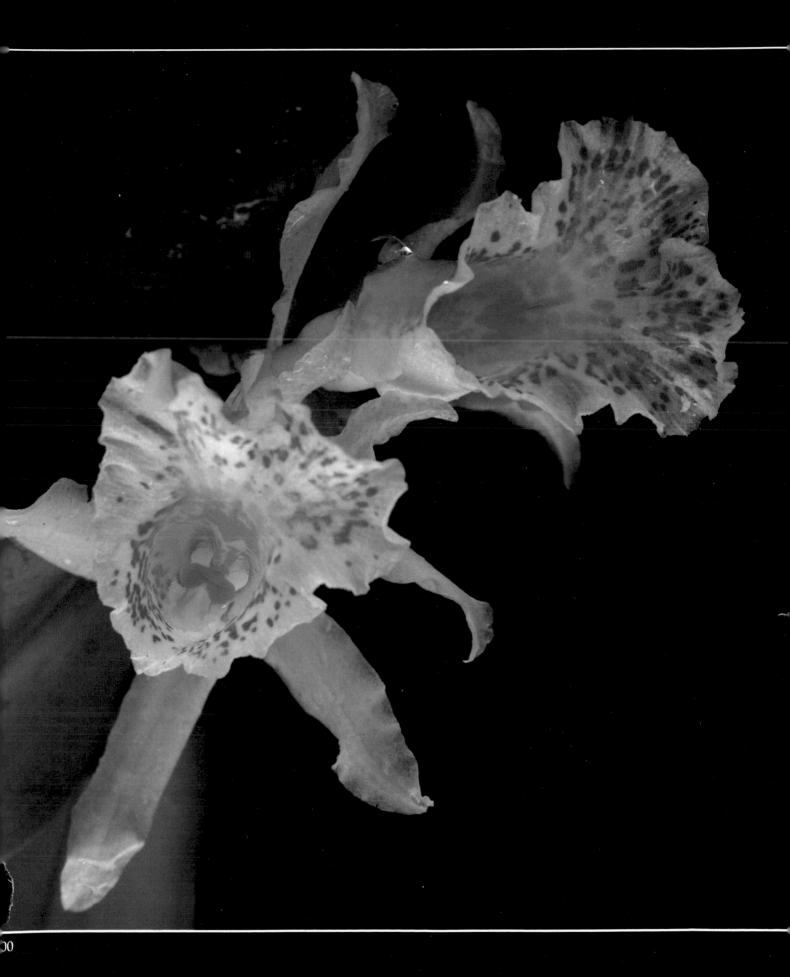

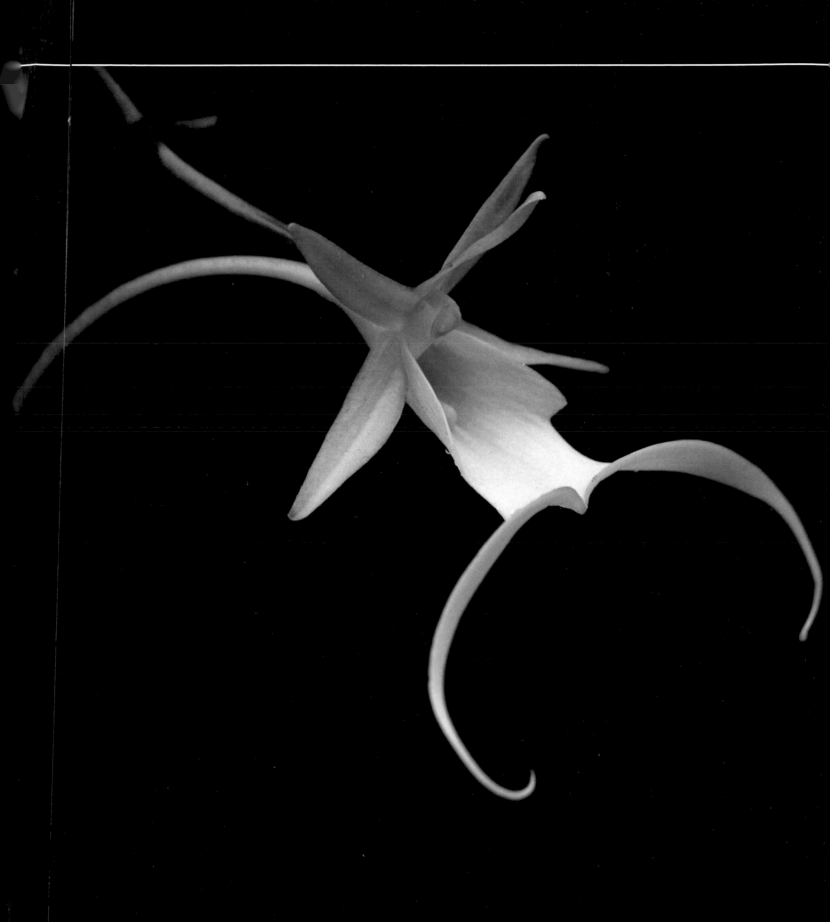

Chiloschista
The name describes the distinctive nature of the split labellum. The seven identified species of these small, leafless, epiphytic orchids can be found in an area stretching from the Himalayas across Southeast Asia and down to Oceania. The multiple roots grow like creepers on the branches of the host tree or shrub and the drooping stalk yields thick groups of small flowers.

Trichoglottis
The name is derived from a combination of the words for fine hair and tongue which reflects the hairy nature of the labellum. The 60 or so species are to be found in the tropics of Asia from the Himalayas to New Guinea. These orchids are climbing epiphytics usually with small fleshy flowers sprouting from the growth sections of the stalks, although some varieties also have flowers growing up the stalks.

Pleurothallis
The name reflects the rib-cage appearance of the closely gathered stems of the plants, coming from a combination of the words rib and sprout or branch. The more than 1000 species are spread over a wide expanse of Central and South America, particularly the Andes region. They are small plants with small flowers. They frequently can be found growing in close proximity rather like mountain grasses.

Liparis
The name, meaning "glistening oil," refers to the glossy appearance of the leaves. These plants are found mainly in the tropics of Asia but also in the temperate and tropical zones of other parts of the world. The 350 or so species are terrestrial or epiphytic. In the temperate zones the upper parts whither and die off in the winter. These orchids are bulbous, producing leaves and plain but delicate flowers.

Microstylis
The name, meaning "small pillar shape," is considered to be a description of the stamen. There are more than 200 species to be found throughout the tropics, especially in India. This genus consists of terrestrial orchids and many of the species are also included in Malaxis. The stalks grow from bulbous roots, and the small flowers are tube-shaped.

Sarcoglottis
The meaning of the name Sarcoglottis, a combination of the words fleshy and tongue, reveals the nature of the fleshy appearance of the labellum. There are something like 50 species growing in Central and South America of this group of large terrestrial orchids. The leaves usually form into a rosettelike shape. The stalks grow upright and support long, slender clusters of blossoms.

Myrmecophila (abbrev. Myrm.)
The name, a combination of the words for ant and love, depicts the fondness that ants have for this genus of orchids because of the suitability of the bulbous roots for making nests. Previously these plants were categorized as a part of Schomburgkia. The plants are large, mainly found in Central America, and are epiphytic.

Coelogyne (abbrev. Coel.)
The name Coelogyne comes from a fusion of the words for cavity and the female sexual organs, alluding to the large hollow found in the stigma. There are more than 120 species growing in the tropics of Asia from the Himalayas and as far down as Oceania. These are epiphytic orchids with one or two leaves growing from bulbous roots. The tips of the stalks yield either single or clustered blooms.

Trichoceros
The name is formed from the combination of the words for hair and tentacle, referring to the hairy antennalike projections coming from both sides of the column. There are about six species to be found in the Andean regions of Colombia, Ecuador, Peru, and Bolivia. They are small, epiphytic orchids with the flowers at the tips of the long stalks resembling insects.

Cyrtopodium
The name, a union of the words for curves and small foot, depicts the characteristics of the column of this group of orchids. The 35 species or so are to be found in the American tropics, especially Brazil. These large, epiphytic plants have thick, heavy stalks and large sword-shaped leaves. The stiffly growing upright stalks divide and support thickly bunched blossoms.

Cryptochilus
The labellum positioned well inside the flower gives this genus its name, which is a combination of the words for hidden and labellum. There are about six species, some of which are epiphytic and some lithophytic. They can be found in Tibet, Nepal, and the Moluccas. They are similar to the orchids of the Elia but the sepals are tube-shaped and the blooms are of a distinctive color.

Sigmatostalix
The name, coming from the words for sigma (C shape) and stem, point to the long, slender column and "C" shaped labellum. About 20 different members of this genus can be found from Mexico to Brazil and Argentina. The plants in this group are small and epiphytic. The blossoms are also small but the labellum opening out at the end of a long stem is distinctive.

Aerangis (abbrev. Aergs.)
The name is a combination of the words for empty space and container which is a reference to the length. About 70 species can be found in tropical Africa, particularly on the island of Madagascar. These plants are epiphytic, small in size and have short stems yielding a few thick leaves. The stalks of the flowers are usually long and downward drooping with a large white flower attached to each.

Warrea
This genus commemorates the name of the flower collector F. Warre. Six different species are to be found over a wide area from Costa Rica to Brazil. The plants are either epiphytic or terrestrial and prefer to grow in high areas. Long, slender, fimbriated leaves sprout from a small bulb and the clusters of flowers grow from an upright stalk.

141. Onc. flexuosum
Brazil, Paraguay and other areas / 2 cm / Summer

142. Chiloschista usneoides
Nepal and Thailand / 1.5 cm / Spring to summer

143. Trichoglottis philippinensis
The islands of the Philippines, mainly Luzon and Mindanao / 3 cm / Spring to summer

144. Pleurothallis cardiostola
Venezuela and Colombia / 2 cm (height) / Winter

145. Liparis sutepensis
Thailand / 1 cm / Early summer

146. Microstylis biloba
The Himalayas, India, Thailand and China / ____ / Late spring

147. Sarcoglottis fasciculata type
Southeast Brazil / 2 cm / Summer

148. Myrm. tibicinis = Schom. tibicinis
From Mexico to Costa Rica / 6 cm / Spring to summer

149. Coel. ovalis
From the Himalayas to Southeast Asia / 4 cm / Summer

150. Trichoceros antennifera
Unknown / ____ / Spring

151. Cyrtopodium punctatum
From Mexico to Argentina / 4-5 cm / Summer

152. Cryptochilus sanguineus
The Himalayas, mainly Nepal / 2.5 cm (length) / Summer

153. Sigmatostalix guatemalensis
Central America / 1-1.5 cm / Winter

154. Aergs. stylosa
Madagascar and the Comoro islands / 3-4 cm / Spring

155. Myrm. tibicinis = Schom. tibicinis
From Mexico to Costa Rica / 6 cm / Spring to summer

156. Warrea costaricensis
Costa Rica and Panama / 5-6 cm / Winter to spring

157. Z. mackai
Brazil / 7 cm / Early winter

158. Grammangis ellisii
Madagascar / 6 cm / Summer

159. Diplocaulobium sp.
____ / ____ / Winter

160. Cyrtorchis monteirae
West Africa from Nigeria to Angola / 3.5 cm / Spring

161. Sarcanthus birmanicus
Sikkim, Burma, Thailand and Vietnam / 1.5 cm / Winter

162. V. coerulea
The Himalayas, Burma and Thailand / 8 cm / Autumn

Grammangis

The words for letter (character type) and receptacle have been combined to give this genus its name, supposedly due to the markings on the labellum. Five species of this large, epiphytic orchid found mainly in Madagascar and other parts of tropical Africa have so far been identified. Leaves grow from the top part of the very large bulbous roots and a considerable number of flowers sprout from the thick stalks.

Diplocaulobium

It is suggested that the name, being a combination of the words for two and stalk, refers to the plants having two kinds of roots. Between 30 and 75 species can be found in a wide area centered on New Guinea stretching as far as the Malay Peninsula, Indonesia, and the Fiji islands. These epiphytic plants were previously included in the *Dendrobium*.

Cyrtorchis

The words "curve" and "mid-height" combine to form the name of this genus due to the petals being folded back. These epiphytic orchids are similar to *Angraecum*. About 15 species can be found in East and South Africa. The stalks can grow upright or hang down. The stiff leaves grow in two rows and the clusters of blossoms are glossy in appearance.

Zygopetalum (abbrev. Z.)

The name is a combination of the words for yoke and petal due to the petals being attached to the thick ring section of the labellum creating a yoke-like shape. There are more than 18 species of this genus of epiphytic and terrestrial orchids growing in all parts of South America. The plants have rounded bulbous roots from which grow leaves with prominent veins and the single flower stalk yields a number of flowers.

Sarcanthus

The name highlights the fleshy nature of the flowers. These plain, epiphytic orchids are to be found in tropical Asia as far afield as the Himalayas and New Guinea. The 90 or so species are characterized by single stalks which can grow upright or hang down. A short labellum and numerous small bag-shaped blossoms grow from a narrow flower stalk.

Stanhopea (abbrev. Stan.)

Stanhope is a person's family name. About 25 different species grow over a wide area from Mexico to Brazil and Peru. They are epiphytic and well known for the flowers being attached to the base of the roots. The bulbs are circular or ovular in shape. The flowers are fleshy but have only a short life.

Vanda (abbrev. V.)

The name comes from the Sanskrit "vandaka," meaning shelter among the trees and shrubs. The more than 70 species are to be found mainly in tropical Asia from the Himalayas down to Oceania. They are epiphytic and the single stalk usually sprouts a ring of leaves arranged in two rows forming a "V" shape. The number of flowers varies from a few to many.

Oncidium (abbrev. Onc.)

The name meaning bulge or protuberance refers to the labellum. Mostly found in tropical America with a total of over 750 species, this is one of the bigger groups of epiphytic orchids with the different species coming in a variety of shapes. Usually the flowers are small and grow thickly together, but there are also many examples of majestically and individually growing blooms. The most distinctive features of this genus are the protruding labellum and the ear-lobe-like attachment to the column.

Odontoglossum (abbrev. Odm.)

The toothlike projections from the base of the labellum give this genus its name. The more than 300 species grow in an area from southern Mexico to Bolivia and grow mainly on high ground such as in the Andes. Many of these epiphytic orchids produce beautiful blooms but they are as yet rarely imported to Japan.

Brassavola (abbrev. B.)

The name comes from the Venetian botanist, A.M. Brassavola. The 20 or more species are native to Central and South America. They are epiphytic and the usually quite sturdy leaves grow thickly together like massed poles. The green and white flowers grow in clusters, the sepals and stamen are thin and the labellum is large. They give off a fragrance at night.

Aspasia

This genus is named after the wife of the great statesman of ancient Greece Pericles. About 10 different species are found from Central America down to Brazil. They are similar to the species of *Odontoglossum*, but the base of the bulb is compressed and the flowers are small and plain.

Trichopilia (abbrev. Trpla.)

The name, a combination of the words for fine hair and felt, describes the tip of the column where a shallow notch appears. There are about 30 members of this genus native to the area from Mexico to Brazil. These densely growing epiphytic orchids often prefer the shade. The bulbous roots produce a single leaf and the short stalk sprouts a relatively large flower or flowers.

Miltonia (abbrev. Milt.)

English name = Pansy orchid

These orchids take their name from the British orchid collector Milton. About 20 species are to be found from Costa Rica down to Brazil. They are epiphytic, and large bloomed variants are often found in the northern parts of South America, particularly in the Andes. They are characterized by the short columns of their flowers and also by the large numbers that open out completely flat.

Phalaenopsis (abbrev. Phal.)

The name describes the similarity of the shape of the blossom to the *Phalaenopsis* species of moth found in tropical regions. The 70 or so types are found in tropical Asia and Oceania. They are epiphytic plants producing single stalks. The stalk is short with a small number of thick leaves attached. The flower stalk usually hangs down yielding either one or a number of blossoms.

163. *Stan.* sp.
____ / ____ / Summer

164. *Onc. papilio*
Venezuela, Colombia, and other areas / 12-15 cm / Irregular

165. *V. roeblingiana*
Unique to the Philippines / 5 cm / Spring to summer

166. *Onc. phymatochilum*
Mexico, Guatemala and Brazil / 3 cm / Spring

167. *Onc. splendidum*
Guatemala, Honduras and other areas / 6-7 cm / Winter to spring

168. *Odm. rossii*
Mexico, Guatemala, Honduras and Nicaragua / 6 cm / Winter to spring

169. *Onc. bicallosum*
Mexico, Guatemala and other areas / 3 × 4 cm / Winter

170. *Odm. majale = Odm. platycheilum*
Highlands in Guatemala / 4 cm / Spring to summer

171. *Odm. chiriquense*
Costa Rica, Panama, Colombia and Peru / 4 cm / Spring

172. *Odm. cordatum*
From Mexico to Costa Rica and Venezuela / 6-7 cm / Summer

173. *B. cucullata*
From Central to northern South America / ____ / Summer

174. *B. digbyana = Ryncholaelia digbyana*
Mexico, Guatemala and other areas / 12-15 cm / Summer

175. *B. nodosa*
From Mexico and Panama to Venezuela / 10 cm / Summer

176. *Aspasia principissa*
Costa Rica and Panama / 6 cm / Spring to summer

177. *Trpla. flagrans*
The West Indies, Venezuela and Colombia / 8 cm / Winter

178. *Phal. mariae*
From northern India to Vietnam / 4-5 cm / Winter to spring

179. *Phal. amboinensis*
The Philippines / 4-5 cm / Summer

180. *Milt. spectabilis*
Brazil / 6 × 8 cm / Spring to summer

181. *Phal. gigantea*
Borneo / 5-6 cm / Winter to spring

182. *Phal. stuartiana*
The Philippines / 5-6 cm / Winter to spring

Kingiella

This genus of orchid takes its name from G. King, the man who conducted an extensive study of Indian orchids. There are about five identified species which can be found over a wide area from India to the Philippines and Indonesia. They are small, epiphytic plants similar to *Phalaenopsis*.

Rhynchostylis (abbrev. *Rhy.*)

The name is a combination of the words for beak and column, and it is thought that the name was arrived at because of the shape of the tip of the column. The four or so varieties are found in the region from India to Southeast Asia. They are single-stalk, epiphytic orchids. The stalk is short and the long, thin, stiff leaves grow in two rows forming a "V" shape. The flower stalk can grow upright or hang down while supporting clusters of waxy flowers.

Thunia

The Bohemian orchid collector Thun Hohenhaim gives his name to this genus. There are about 10 species which can be found in the Himalayas, North India, Burma, and Thailand. They are terrestrial and prefer growing on high ground. Two rows of deciduous leaves grow out from the upright stalk, rather like a pond reed, but a graceful bloom sprouts from the tip.

Aerides (abbrev. *Aer.*)

The name is derived from the word for air, reflecting the epiphytic nature of this genus consisting of about 60 species. They can be found across a wide part of tropical Asia including Japan, China, and New Guinea. They are characterized by single stalks and are in the main similar to *Vanda*, but the flower stalks hang down and there are a number of them that exhibit large numbers of glossy flowers.

Doritis

The name, meaning spear, is probably a reference to the shape of the labellum although it is also thought, by some, to come from the goddess Aphrodite. From one to three different species can be found across India and Southeast Asia. These epiphytic orchids are similar to those in *Phalaenopsis*. A number of leaves grow out from the short stalk in two rows and the small flowers grow from the erect flower stalks like heads of grain.

Calanthe (abbrev. *Cal.*)

A combination of the words for beautiful and flower gives this genus its name. Mainly found in the temperate and tropical zones of Asia, but also seen in Africa and parts of Central and South America. There are more than 150 species of these orchids which are usually classified into two main categories: temperate evergreens and tropical deciduous.

Cymbidium (abbrev. *Cym.*)

The shape of the labellum is the basis for the name which means ship or cup shape. The 70 or so species are to be found over a very wide area from the temperate zone of Asia, including Japan, through Southeast Asia, and down to Oceania. They can be terrestrial or epiphytic. Some of the spring orchids of the temperate zones have been cultivated from ancient times in China and Japan.

Sophronitis (abbrev. *Soph.*)

The name, meaning purity and modesty, appears to allude to the hidden nature of the anther on one side of the column. It is believed to be confined to Brazil and there are only six or seven known species of these small, epiphytic orchids, although this number does vary according to different authorities. The flowers are large compared with the roots and because of their vivid colors they are very popular with gardeners and horticulturists.

Polyrrhiza

The name directly points to the densely growing roots of this genus. The four identified species are to be found in South Florida and the West Indies. They are leafless, epiphytic orchids. The roots grow on the branches and greenery of trees in very humid wooded areas. A stalk grows from the center from which sprouts one or a number of blossoms.

Barkeria

The British horticulturist G. Barker gives his name to this genus of orchids. There are more than 14 species which grow in Mexico and other parts of Central America. These epiphytic plants are very similar to those of *Epidendrum*. Thick leaves grow randomly on the tube-shaped stalk with the blooms growing from the tips. The roots are thick and grow together densely.

183. *Milt. phalaenopsis*
Colombia / 5-6 cm / Spring to summer

184. *Phal. cornu-cervi*
Burma, Thailand, the Malay Peninsula and Indonesia / 4-5 cm / Summer

185. *Kingiella decumbens = Phalaenopsis decumbens*
From southern India to Malaysia and the Philippines / 1 cm / Mainly summer

186. *Phal. mannii*
The Philippines and Borneo / 4-5 cm / Summer

187. *Aer. japonicum*
The western coasts of the Izushichi islands and the main island of Okinawa in Japan / 3 cm / Early summer

188. *Phal. amabilis*
From Taiwan and the Philippines down to Australia / 8-10 cm / Spring

189. *Rhy. coelestis* var. *alba*
Thailand / 2 cm / Summer to autumn

190. *Thunia marshalliana*
India and Burma / 12 cm / Early summer

191. *Doritis pulcherrima*
Southeast Asia / 2-3 cm / Autumn to winter

192. *Aer. mitratum*
Burma, Thailand and Laos / 2 cm / Summer

193. *Doritis pulcherrima*
Southeast Asia / 2-3 cm / Autumn to winter

194. *Cal. furcata*
From Malaysia to the Islands of Southern Kyushu / 5 cm / Summer to autumn

195. *Cal. cardioglossa*
Thailand and Vietnam / 3 cm / Winter

196. *Cal. discolor*
In Japan from the southwest of Hokkaido down to Kyushu and Okinawa / 2-3 cm / Late spring

197. *Cym. lowianum*
Burma and India (the plains of Cashia) / 10 cm / Spring

198. *Cym. kanran*
Japan, China and Taiwan / about 10 cm / Late autumn

199. *Trpla. tortilis*
Mexico, Guatemala, and Honduras / 8-10 cm / Spring

200. *Trpla. suavis*
From Costa Rica to Colombia / 10 cm / Spring

201. *Soph. rosea = Soph. wittigiana*
Brazil (the northern part of Espírito Santo) / 6-7 cm / Winter

202. *Polyrrhiza lindeni*
South Florida and Cuba / 6 × 10 cm / Irregular

203. *Barkeria skinneri*
Mexico and Guatemala / 3 cm / Autumn to winter

Postscript

This collection of photographs is being published to commemorate the 12th World Orchid Conference in Japan, and came about because of my association with the WOC, occasioned by the publication of my previous collection of photographs, *The Orchid* (1975). The exhibition of photographs from that book happened to become a commemorative exhibition at the 8th World Orchid Conference in Thailand.

The World Orchid Conference is held once every three years and has two main purposes: it provides an opportunity for orchid lovers to gather socially, and it allows the exchange of scholarly information. The discussions are divided into those which concern wild varieties and those concerning horticultural varieties, and the orchids are displayed in these categories.

Because of this, I felt that the commemorative collection of photographs should reflect these characteristics. It seemed to me that, compared with the horticultural varieties, the wild varieties, some of which have survived for nearly two hundred million years, have a vital and tenacious energy, and the very dramatic shapes of the flowers make them excellent subjects for photographs.

In the previous book, a large-format camera was used to emphasize texture, and the flowers were arranged by genus and species. It was intended as a photographic encyclopedia of orchids. In this book, it was my intention to make the best use of the sensitivity which some say characterizes many of my photographs. I tried to make sensitivity the essence, tempered with reason. I am best known as a photographer of women, and I tried to compose the book around the idea of using orchids to suggest a woman's life. A large number of wild orchids have an anthropomorphic quality, and there was no shortage of subjects on this theme. However, when I began to compose the scenario, I realized the difficulties. Unless many examples of the same variety are displayed together, the individuality of orchids does not seem to come out fully; but photographing crowds of orchids seemed an unreasonable alternative. And no matter how much effort is given to categorization, some specialists will insist that some species be differently grouped. It was essential to consider expert opinion before deciding which role each orchid should play.

I would like to convey my deepest thanks to all the people who have helped me in the compilation of this book: it would not have been the same without their full cooperation and dedication.

Takashi Kijima